Look - Book 1

By Viola & Zaida Stefano

A catalogue record of this book is available from the **National Library of Australia.**

ISBN: 978-0-6456272-3-7

Authors: Viola Stefano & Zaida Stefano
Illustrations, photographs, cover & internal designs: Zaida Stefano

Disclaimer: The content presented in this book is meant for educational purposes only. The authors & publisher claim no accountability to any entity or person for any liability, damage, or loss caused or assumed to be caused directly or indirectly as a consequence of the application, use, or interpretation of the material in this book.

VeeZee Publications

First published in Australia in 2023
by VeeZee Publications Pty Ltd
veezeepublications.com

Learning made easy with

VeeZee!

Focus Core words in 'Look - Book 1' and the 'Look' series	Secondary Core words in 'Look - Book 1' and the 'Look' series	Other secondary Core words in the 'Look' series but **NOT** in 'Look - Book 1'

Core Vocabulary used throughout **VeeZee Publications**

I	want	can	stop	look
like	more	he	go	see
here	what	do	the	and
out	where	we	it	up
not	they	when	that	down
she	now	them	is	put
help	off	you	yes	on
turn	who	this	no	why
done	make	a	to	under
come	in	some	which	there
open	get	good	same	home

All Core word readers through the various ranges in VeeZee Publications have been developed around specific themes. The themed photos and illustrations present a backdrop for the Core words used in each book. Your students are exploring and interpreting the messages conveyed by these images. They are learning to consider the text in order to understand the images. They are therefore making links between images and the corresponding texts. You are using a range of Core words when discussing the photos and illustrations with your students, specifically; who, what, where, when and why. The use of these 'question' words in discussion further reinforces their meanings and their associations with surrounding words. We recommend that students without a vision impairment also explore the readers designed for students with low vision. This will support interaction and discussion amongst the students. It is our hope that this will ultimately promote acceptance, understanding, compassion and teamwork, thus cultivating true inclusion.

We hope you have fun discovering what animals are in our 'Look' books. Not all of our animals have been named, so good luck with your research!

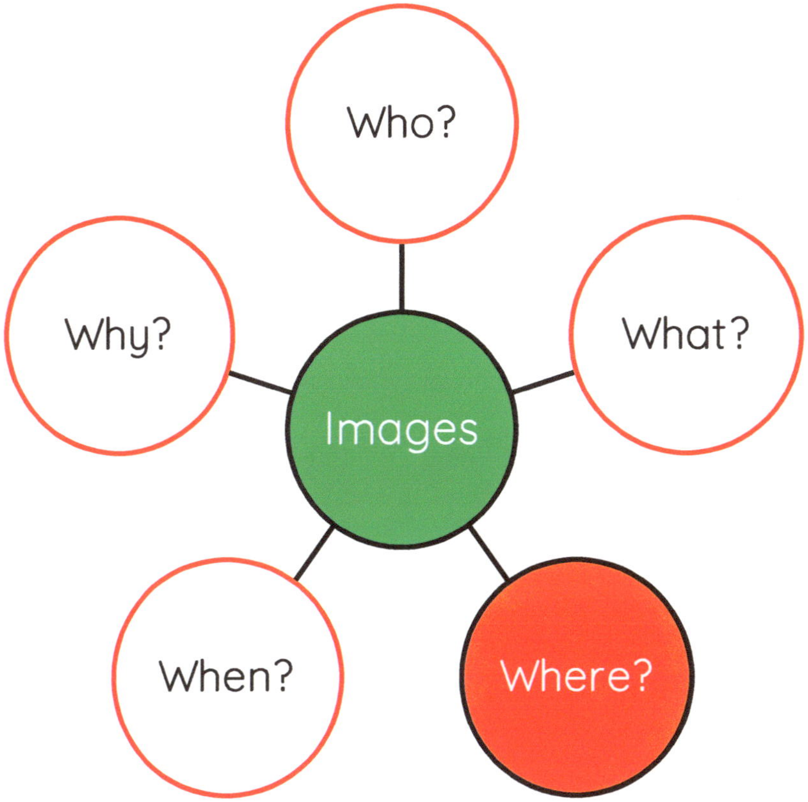
Who?
Why?
What?
Images
When?
Where?

Where do tigers live?

Look.

Look here.

Look there.

Look now.

Look here now.

Look there now.

Come look mum.

Come look dad.

Come look here mum and dad.

Look there mum and dad.

Look at them.

Look at them now.

Look at them now, mum and dad.

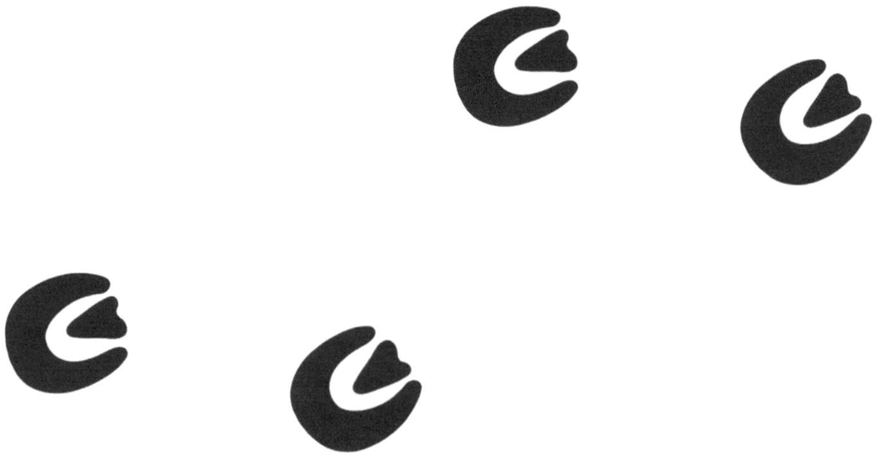

We can look at them here.

We can look at them there.

Look at them here, and
look at them there.

Words in this book

here	at	come
there	look	mum

Words in this book

them	now	and
we	dad	can

Do you know the focus and secondary Core words: 'look' , 'here' and 'now'? Read the words along each line.						
look	look	here	now	look	now	look
here	look	look	now	here	look	now
now	look	now	look	look	here	now
now	look	look	now	here	look	now
look	here	now	look	look	here	look
here	look	here	now	look	look	now
look	now	here	look	here	now	look

Do you know the focus and secondary Core words in this book (refer to Core word table)? Find them along each line, point to them and say them. Read the other words too once you have pointed to the Core words.						
look	here	mum	there	look	now	can
at	and	there	now	mum	here	come
there	look	now	look	here	we	dad
now	mum	here	and	them	at	look
here	dad	now	mum	look	come	there
dad	come	look	here	we	mum	now
mum	now	there	can	now	look	here

How many times did you read the word 'look'?

Make new words with '___ow', e.g., 'slow'. Write sentences using these words.

We hope you had fun reading!

www.ingramcontent.com/pod-product-compliance
Lightning Source LLC
Chambersburg PA
CBHW050853010526
44107CB00047BA/1590
9780645627237